WILDERNESS ADVENTURES

Camping

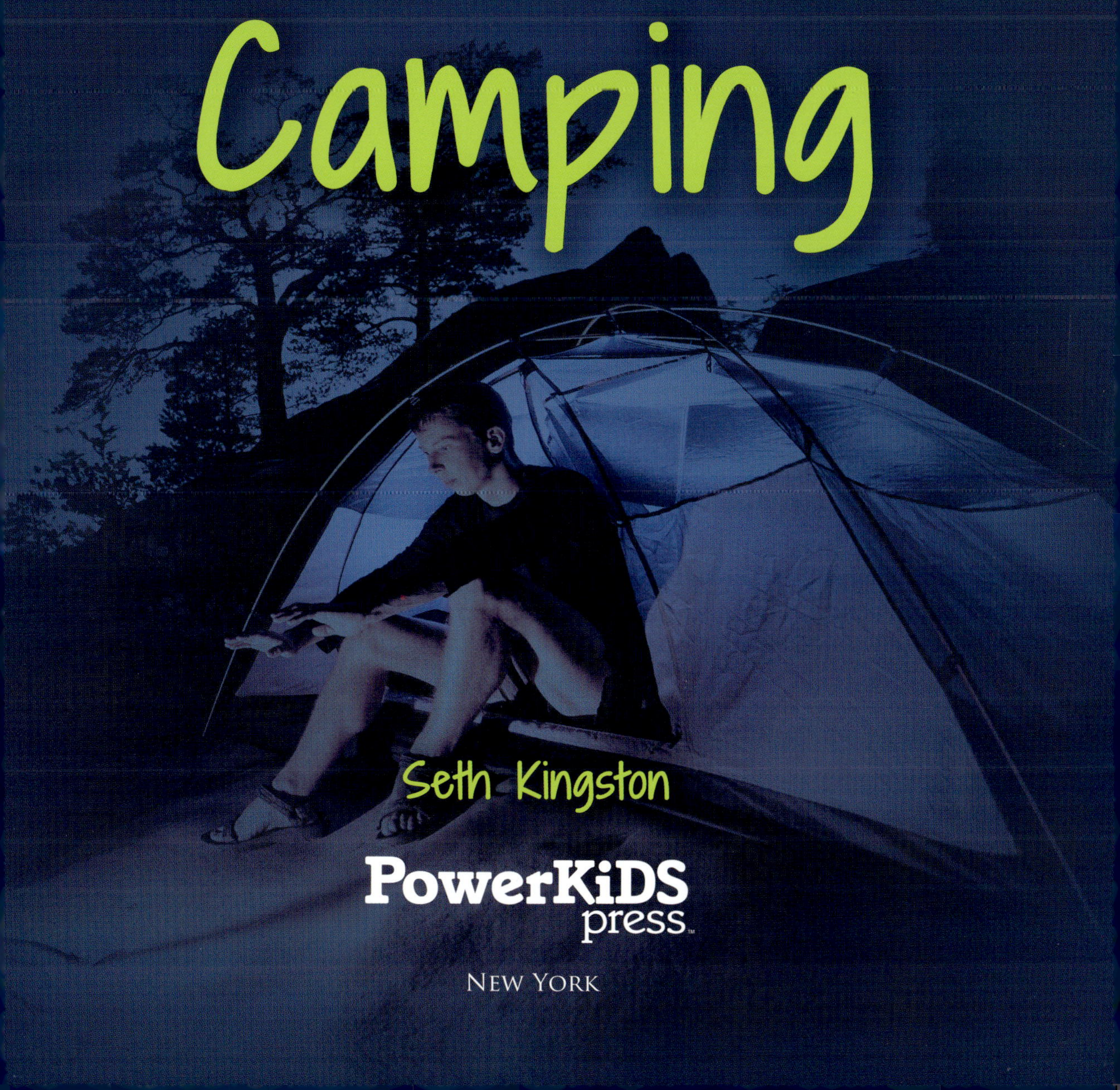

Seth Kingston

PowerKiDS press.

NEW YORK

Published in 2022 by The Rosen Publishing Group, Inc.
29 East 21st Street, New York, NY 10010

First Edition

Portions of this work were originally authored by Suzanne Slade and published as *Let's Go Camping.* All new material in this edition was authored by Seth Kingston.

Editor: Caitie McAneney
Book Design: Michael Flynn

Photo Credits: Cover, p. 5 (main) (camper) anatoliy_gleb/Shutterstock.com; cover, pp. 7, 15, 27, 29 (mountain logo) doyz86/Shutterstock.com; interior (mountain background) Lidiia/Shutterstock.com; p. 5 (inset) PeopleImages/E+/Getty Images; p. 6 Akcamczuk/iStock/Getty Images; p. 7 Jordan Siemens/Stone/Getty Images; p. 8 Vesnaandjic/E+/Getty Images; p. 9 LisaBrightfire/iStock/Getty Images; p. 10 rukawajung/iStock/Getty Images; p. 11 Maxwell Frank/Getty Images; p. 12 mikroman6/Momen/Getty Images; p. 13 Edwin Remsberg/The Image Bank/Getty Images; p. 15 Maya Karkalicheva/Moment/Getty Images; p. 17 Thomas Barwick/DigitalVision/Getty Images; p.18 Yurii_Yarema/Shutterstock.com; p. 19 visualspace/E+/Getty Images; p. 20 Linda Parton/Shutterstock.com; p. 21 Stefan Wackerhagen/Getty Images; p. 22 mixetto/E+/Getty Images; p. 23 Fuse/Corbis/Getty Images; p. 24 Yana Bukharov/Moment/Getty Images; p. 25 Elsa Amsterdam/Shutterstock.com; p. 27 Laura Hedien/Moment/Getty Images; p 29 SerrNovik/iStock/Getty Images.

Library of Congress Cataloging-in-Publication Data

Names: Kingston, Seth, author.
Title: Camping / Seth Kingston.
Description: New York : PowerKids Press, [2022] | Series: Wilderness adventures | Includes index.
Identifiers: LCCN 2020039403 | ISBN 9781725329232 (library binding) | ISBN 9781725329218 (paperback) | ISBN 9781725329225 (6 pack)
Subjects: LCSH: Camping--Juvenile literature.
Classification: LCC GV191.7 .K52 2022 | DDC 796.54--dc23
LC record available at https://lccn.loc.gov/2020039403

Manufactured in the United States of America

Some of the images in this book illustrate individuals who are models. The depictions do not imply actual situations or events.

Note to Parents and Teachers: Some of the activities in this book require adult supervision. Please talk with your child or student before allowing them to proceed with any wilderness activities.

CPSIA Compliance Information: Batch #CWPK22. For further information contact Rosen Publishing, New York, New York at 1-800-237-9932.

CONTENTS

The Great Outdoors

Have you ever wanted to live in the great outdoors? Have you ever wanted to sleep under the stars? You might live in a busy city or a **suburb** full of houses, but you can always go camping.

Camping is a great opportunity to explore nature. You can discover different kinds of animals and see how they live in the wild. You can hike through a forest, climb a mountain, or swim in a lake. Watch for bats taking flight at sunset. Listen for hooting owls or howling coyotes. You can see hundreds of twinkling stars away from the city lights. You'll find many challenges while camping, like setting up your tent, but it's always worth it to "rough it" in the wild!

Search the night sky for **constellations** or look for the bright North Star.

Campground Fun

Campgrounds are places set aside for people to camp, and they usually have all you need for a fun camping trip. Many state and national parks have campgrounds. These campgrounds usually have bodies of water for swimming and fishing, hiking trails, playgrounds, and bathrooms. Choose a camping location that offers the types of activities your family enjoys. Parks have a certain number of campsites. During the summer months, campsites at popular campgrounds often fill up quickly. You should book your campsite before you leave home.

Some campsites are simple and **remote**, without showers, toilets, or running water. Others have places for you to shower, shop for supplies, and even wash clothes. Many families want a campsite with at least a water pump and firepit.

NATIONAL PARKS

You can camp in national parks all over the United States. More than 400 national park sites make up the U.S. National Park System. Around 130 parks offer camping, from Denali National Park in Alaska to Everglades National Park in Florida. You can camp in a campground with **amenities** like bathrooms. Or, you can make your adventure a little wilder by camping in the backcountry, or far from a campground.

WILD FILE

Some hikers camp overnight on long backpacking hikes. They might spend the night in a **hammock**, under the stars, or in a lean-to—a simple open shelter with a sloping roof.

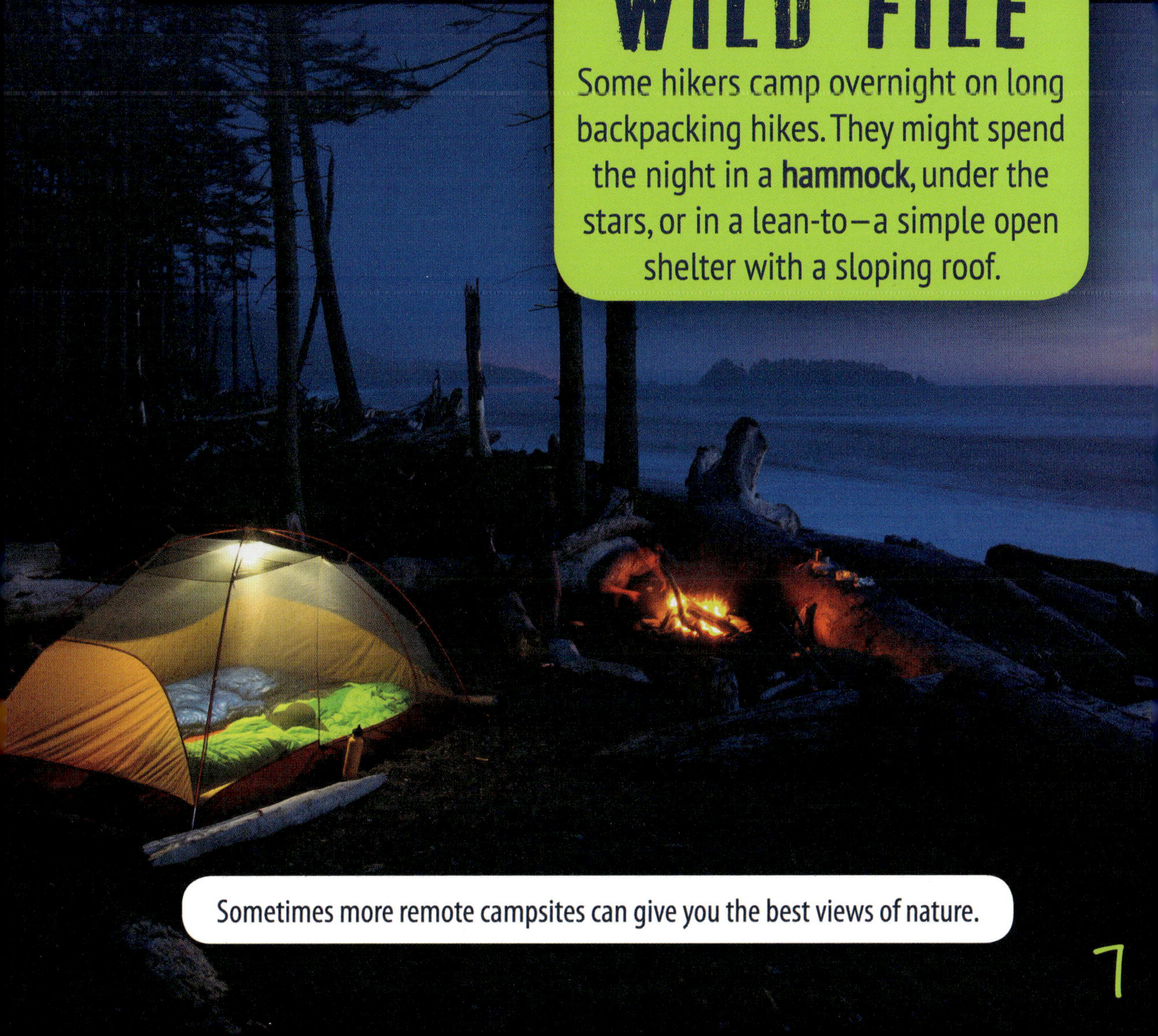

Sometimes more remote campsites can give you the best views of nature.

Tent Camping

Imagine you want to try tent camping. Which tent is right for your family? Some people like small, simple tents, while others prefer larger tents with lots of features. Small tents are easier to carry on backpacking trips. Bigger tents can comfortably fit your family and serve as a home away from home.

Tents vary in size from small, one-person tents to large tents that hold six to eight people.

There are three basic kinds of tents. An A-frame tent has two sloping sides that meet at a pointed top. A dome tent has a rounded shape. The third type of tent is a cabin tent. It looks like a house with four straight walls and an angled roof. Some large tents have cloth walls that divide the tent into several rooms. Some even have closets for your gear!

Pitch Your Tent!

Once you arrive at your campsite, it's time to pitch your tent. Before setting up your tent, clear the area of rocks and sticks. Make sure the ground is dry. Most tents are easy to set up. Thin, flexible poles hold a tent up. The poles slide through loops on the outside of the tent. You can fasten your tent to the ground with stakes.

Set up your sleeping area in your tent and store your gear. Then, get it ready for the weather. If it's hot out, you can open up any tent windows for airflow. Many tents have a screen that lets air in but keeps bugs out. If it might rain, you can put a **rainfly** over your tent to protect it.

WILD FILE

Some tents have a window in the roof, called a skylight. This lets light in and allows you to see the stars at night. It also might have a screen to keep bugs away.

It's always smart to pitch your tent while the sun is still up. Then you can see all the parts. Always bring the instructions for your tent, just in case!

Plan Ahead

You won't have all the comforts of home while you're camping. It's important to plan ahead to know what you'll need on your trip. You can go camping for several weeks or plan a short overnight trip. Most campers stay in a tent or cabin. Others stay in a **recreational** vehicle, or RV.

WILD FILE

A basic first aid kit has bandages of different sizes, **sterile** wipes and pads, and **antibiotic** ointment, or cream.

You need to pack things for sleep, like sleeping bags, cots, and pillows. Pack things to eat, like snacks, water, and foods you can cook over a campfire. Pack essentials like sunscreen, bug spray, and a first aid kit. Make sure to pack your recreational gear, too! You can bring bikes to explore trails. You can bring canoes, kayaks, and fishing gear to spend time on the water. You can bring a hammock to set up between two trees for reading.

RVs often have some comforts of home, like electricity and beds, and sometimes even a bathroom and kitchen. Camping in an RV can be like taking your home with you on a trip!

Prepared for Anything

You might imagine a sunny, perfect day for your camping trip. However, you can't control the weather. Check the weather **forecast** for the area before you leave. That can give you an idea of how to prepare for the weather.

Rain can put a damper on camping if you're not prepared. Be sure to pitch your tent on high ground so water will run away from your tent. Pack an umbrella so you can stay dry if you go outside. If winds become strong, place large rocks over the tent stakes to keep your tent from blowing away. Remember to pack some books and games in case you need to spend a rainy day inside your tent. Pack clothes and gear to prepare for both the warmest and coldest temperatures of your trip.

LIGHTNING SAFETY

What if a storm rolls through your campsite? You have to take shelter quickly. If possible, get into an all-metal car or building. Tents and lean-tos can't protect you. If shelter isn't available, go to a low-lying area, such as a ditch. Don't take cover under trees. Don't hike up peaks or in wide-open spaces when there's a thunderstorm in the forecast. Wait at least 30 minutes after the storm to leave your shelter.

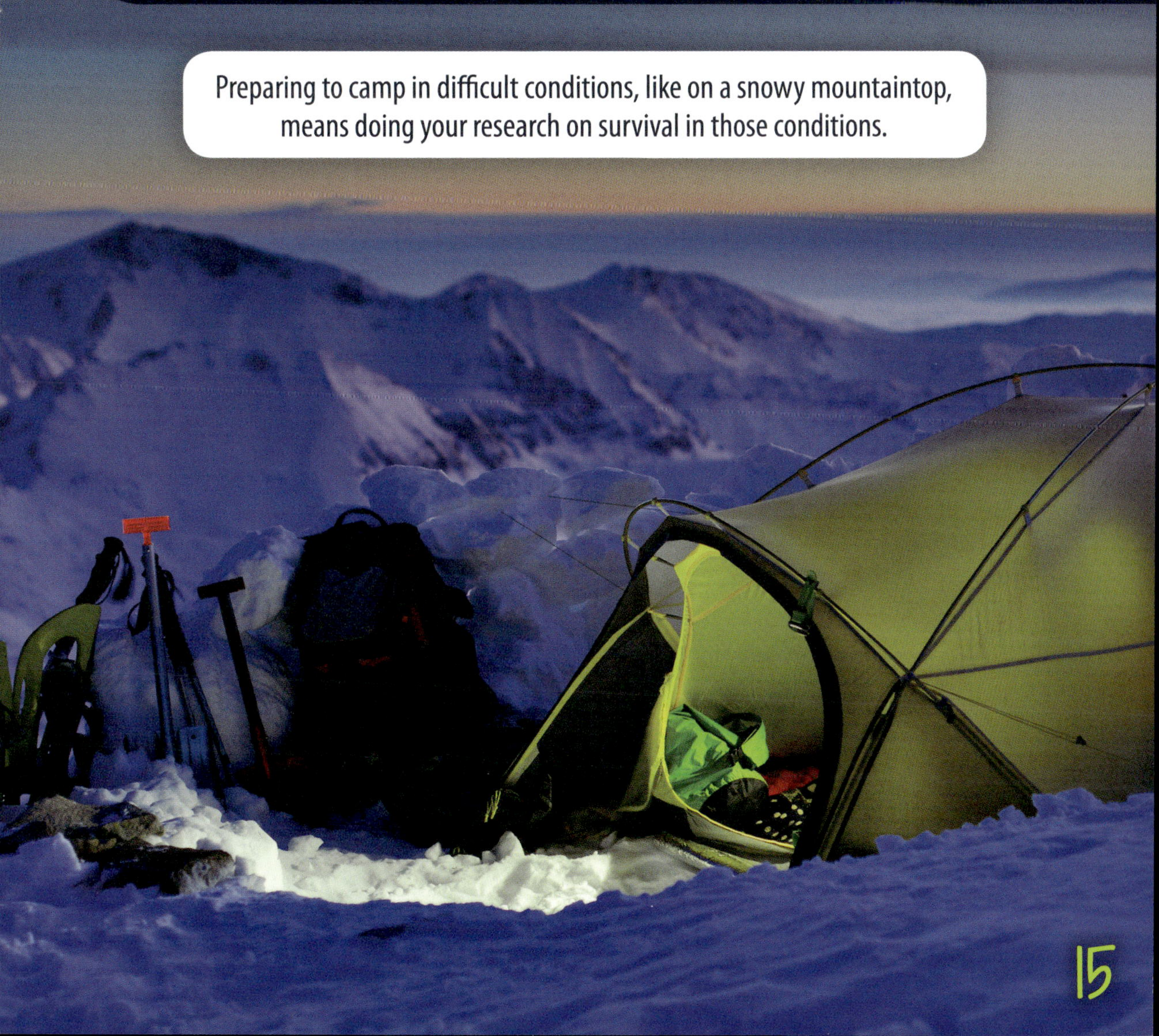

Preparing to camp in difficult conditions, like on a snowy mountaintop, means doing your research on survival in those conditions.

Camping Clothes

Camping is more comfortable when you pack the right clothing. You probably won't have air conditioning or heating, like you do at home. Check the weather report before leaving home, so you will know the right type of clothing to pack.

It is helpful to dress in layers. If the day gets warmer, you can quickly adapt to the weather. Many campers and hikers choose to wear **synthetic** fabrics like polyester or natural fabrics like wool. These can keep you warm when it's cold and cool when it's hot. Also, these fabrics don't stay wet for too long. You should have boots or sneakers to protect your feet while you hike. Choose the right backpack to fit everything you need to wear and carry.

WILD FILE

Many campers and hikers avoid wearing cotton, especially in cold weather. When cotton gets wet, it stays wet for a while, which can cause **hypothermia**.

Choosing the right clothes is just as important as choosing the right shelter. Remember that it gets colder at night, and it's always smart to pack a coat and hat.

Making a Fire

Making a campfire is one of the best parts of camping. You can use a fire to stay warm in colder weather or at night. You can also use a fire to cook food and heat water. But first, you have to learn how to make the fire.

First, put dry, crushed paper in the center of your campsite's firepit. Then place small, dry sticks around the paper in an upright position. Ask an adult to light the paper with matches or a lighter. After the sticks begin to burn, add larger logs around the fire. Always keep a bucket of water nearby in case you need to put out your fire. Never leave a fire unattended, or without someone watching it.

Campfires are useful for heating water and food. Remember to pack cooking tools like pots, pans, and a teapot.

Cook with Fire!

There's nothing like cooking food over a campfire! Campers often cook simple foods that are easy to pack, store, and heat up. There are many simple dishes you can make over a campfire.

WILD FILE

Simple pies baked in pie irons over a fire are sometimes called "mountain pies."

Some of the easiest foods to cook over a fire are hot dogs or marshmallows on a stick. You can also heat baked beans in a pot. Some people put foods like vegetables and hamburger meat in a foil pouch and place it in the hot coals. Some campers put bread and fillings—like apples or pizza toppings—into pie irons and cook them over the fire. A popular camping dessert is s'mores—roasted marshmallows, chocolate, and graham crackers. Each family often has their own favorite camping food traditions.

If you have a frying pan, you can fry eggs and bacon for breakfast, or hamburgers and potatoes for lunch.

Gather Round

Campfires are great for cooking, but they can also be a special place to gather. Campers often gather around a campfire at the end of the day. You can enjoy your friends, family, and the warmth of a glowing fire as you relax after a day filled with fun camping activities. Many campers tell campfire stories—even scary stories! Others talk about their adventures in nature or interesting plants and animals they saw.

Put food along a skewer, or long stick, to cook it over the fire.

Many people enjoy singing songs around the campfire. Some people even bring along an instrument to play, such as a guitar or harmonica. Well-known campfire songs include "Down by the Bay," "The Bear Went Over the Mountain," and "I Met a Bear." Do you know any fun campfire songs?

Roast marshmallows and tell stories around a crackling fire.

Neighbors in Nature

At home, you might have plenty of human neighbors. You respect their space and their privacy. In nature, your neighbors are the animals that call that area home. Animals are very interesting to observe, but they deserve space and respect.

You should also be careful around animals in the wild. Never approach or corner an animal. It might get scared and attack you. When walking through the woods, watch the trail for snakes. Some snakes will bite, and some are **venomous**. Animals such as raccoons and bears have a great sense of smell. Don't leave food lying out. Store all food in closed containers or in a car, not just in your tent. Animals can rip a hole in a tent to get to your food!

Some campers put their food in a special container. They hang it from a tree where animals can't reach it.

Respect for Nature

Camping is all about enjoying nature. However, campers have to take care of nature too. Most campgrounds are wonderful places to visit because campers take good care of them. A common rule of camping is "leave no trace." Take everything out of the campground that you brought in. Don't leave any trash or food scraps behind.

Campers also must respect plants. They know it is best not to pick flowers or berries. They leave them for other people to see or animals to eat. Campers do not break off living branches to build a fire. They don't step on plants, especially those that are in danger of dying out. When campers take care of nature, they can keep campgrounds beautiful for future campers.

BEAR WITH ME

North America is home to grizzly bears and black bears. Grizzly bears are found in western U.S. states like Wyoming, Washington, Idaho, and Montana, as well as Canada and Alaska. Grizzly bears are top predators, but attacks are rare–only about one per year in the wilderness. Black bears are a bit smaller and much more common. They can be found around campsites in around 40 U.S. states, Canada, and Mexico. They also rarely attack, but it's still important to keep your distance.

Plants and animals live together in a food web in nature. It's important not to **disrupt** this food web with litter or harm to living things.

Try Something New!

Do you want to try new outdoor activities? Camping might be the perfect vacation for you. Many campgrounds have special areas where you can learn to climb, swim, sail, and canoe. Some have instructors who teach campers how to ride a horse or shoot arrows with a bow. Other campgrounds offer art classes, such as painting or drawing. There are also plenty of activities to do on your own. You can hike with a friend or fish in a lake.

There's always something new to see and do while camping. Spend your days hiking or fishing. Cook out over a fire. Sing songs and tell stories with your friends and families. Fall asleep to the sounds of crickets. Explore all that nature has to offer!

SAFETY TIPS

- Use the buddy system. Hike with a friend!
- Bring plenty of water on long hikes.
- Never approach a wild animal.
- Never leave a campfire unattended.
- Seek appropriate shelter during a storm.
- Pack appropriate clothing and gear for all possible weather conditions.
- Research your camping area to learn about possible risks.
- Always listen to information and warnings from campground and park staff.

Some campgrounds allow you to try rock climbing, a fun and challenging outdoor activity.

GLOSSARY

amenity: Something that helps provide comfort and enjoyment.

antibiotic: A drug that can kill germs, including harmful bacteria.

constellation: A collection of stars that seem to make up a certain shape.

disrupt: To affect in a way that causes something to be unable to continue in its usual way.

forecast: An informed guess about future weather.

hammock: A swinging bed made of cloth or netting.

hypothermia: Dangerously low body temperature caused by cold conditions.

rainfly: A large sheet that covers a tent to keep it safe from rain or sun.

recreational: Something done for pleasure or relaxation.

remote: Far away.

sterile: Free from germs.

suburb: A smaller community next to a city.

synthetic: Man-made; not found in nature.

venomous: Able of put poison or venom into another animal's body.

FOR MORE INFORMATION

Books

Siber, Kate. *National Parks of the U.S.A.* Minneapolis, MN: Wide Eyed Editions, 2018.

Towell, Colin. *Survival for Beginners: A Step-by-Step Guide to Camping and Outdoor Skills.* London, UK: DK Publishing, 2019.

Websites

10 Black Bear Facts!
www.natgeokids.com/uk/discover/animals/general-animals/black-bear-facts/
Learn more about one common animal you might find while camping—the black bear.

How to Build Your Campfire
smokeybear.com/en/prevention-how-tos/campfire-safety/how-to-build-your-campfire
Learn how to build a campfire with Smokey Bear!

INDEX